To Ralph
—DB

To Irene
—MD

With special thanks to Ann Stewart
of the Leiber Collection

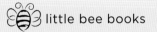 little bee books

251 Park Avenue South, New York, NY 10010
Text copyright © 2019 by Deborah Blumenthal
Illustrations copyright © 2019 by Masha D'yans
All rights reserved, including the right of reproduction
in whole or in part in any form.
Library of Congress Cataloging-in-Publication Data is available upon request
Manufactured in China   TPL 0819
First Edition   10 9 8 7 6 5 4 3 2 1
ISBN 978-1-4998-0898-8

littlebeebooks.com

PARROTS, PUGS, AND PIXIE DUST

A Book About Fashion Designer
Judith Leiber

WORDS:
DEBORAH BLUMENTHAL

ART:
MASHA D'YANS

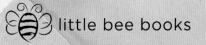

little bee books

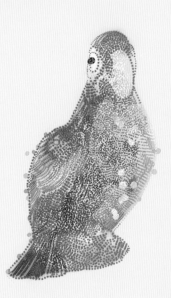

For animal lovers
there are preening peacocks,
fanciful frogs donning gilded crowns,
pandas, poodles, parrots, pugs,
and even rattlesnakes.

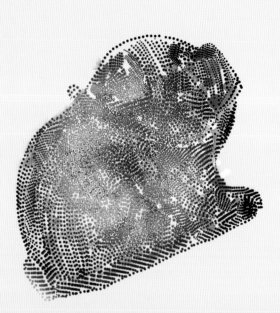

For fast foodies—
burgers and fries,
pears, pineapples, ice pops,
and layer cake.

But things aren't always what they seem.

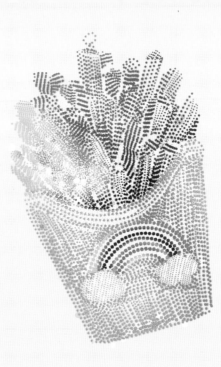

Don't pet these pugs
or bite the burgers.
These jazzy creations are . . . evening bags!

And Judith Leiber designed them all.

Her happily-ever-after world of purses
for Cinderella balls
sparkled with candy-colored gemstones
and a pinch of pixie dust,
so they called her
the Queen of Minaudières*—
a fancy French word for
jewel-like handbags.

*Minaudières is pronounced mee-nohd-YAIRZ.

"I just thought it was a good idea
to make something strange
that we'd never made before," Judith said.

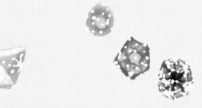

So she turned
ordinary
into extraordinary,
gluing tiny crystals,
one
by
one—
up to 13,000 on each bag—
until they twinkled like fireflies.

Judith was born on July 11, 1921, in Hungary.
Her fashion passion
was inspired by her dad, Emil Peto.
Whenever he traveled,
he would bring her mom, Helene,
a special handbag.

Her mom loved them,
and so did Judith,
who decided,
"I am going to do that."

Her ideas came from . . . well . . . everywhere,
including some that came from . . . who knows where?

Like polka-dot pigs,
crystal turtles,
and shimmering teapots!

Dreaming of posh dress-up bags
helped Judith cope
with her hard life.
She grew up in Budapest,
at a time when Jewish families like hers
were treated cruelly,
just because they were Jewish.

An aunt made face creams,
so her parents thought she should, too.
In 1938, when she was just seventeen,
she left for London to study chemistry.

A year later, she came home for vacation
but never went back to school.
War broke out,
and she wanted to be near
her parents and sister, Eva.

She found a trainee spot at a handbag house—
where she was the only girl—
and through 1943, Judith learned the business
from the bottom up,
starting with sweeping floors.

But by the time she was ready for a real job,
Jewish people were being taken away.

Judith's family was luckier than most.
They were spared,
but made to work
sewing army uniforms.
At night, she took comfort
in making handbags
with any scraps she could find.

Life got harder as the war went on.
Judith's family was crowded into a small apartment
with other Jewish families.
Then they were forced
to hide out in a dark basement.

When the war ended in the springtime of 1945,
they finally went home.

A year later Judith met
Gerson Leiber,
an American soldier.

"It was love at first sight," he said.

In 1947, they sailed
on a "bride ship,"
a boat for American servicemen
and their new European wives,
to New York City, their new home.

After working for other handbag companies,
Judith started her own business in 1963.
Gerson, called Gus,
a painter and sculptor,
helped her run it.

"I knew from the beginning
what I was going to do," she said.
"I was going to make the best."

But the best
began
with the worst.

When a metal handbag Judith designed
came back from Italy,
the bottom had turned slime green.

But sometimes big mistakes
make wrongs go right.

She didn't toss it out.
She didn't start over.

She hid the green
under shimmering crystals,
and it was a hit!

Dashing divas
sought out Judith's bags—
even the wives of presidents.

When Dwight D. Eisenhower became president in 1953,
First Lady Mamie's "jewel in hand" for the inaugural balls
was adorned with pearls and rhinestones.
It matched her sherbet-pink, peau-de-soie gown.

When Ronald Reagan became president in 1981,
Nancy Reagan's Leiber bag
was white silk and silver crystal.

Almost every first lady since has carried one.
Barbara Bush's resembled her springer spaniel, Millie.
Hillary Clinton's looked like Socks, the family cat.

Perhaps most memorable
was a bag made not for a president's wife:
(though it should have been):
the white dove with an olive branch.
On its side, glittering rhinestones
brightly spelled out P-E-A-C-E
in English, French,
Hebrew, and Arabic.

Judith kept designing bags until 1998.
Then she and Gus
started a museum in East Hampton, New York,
to display their work.

Gus was ninety-six years old
when he died at home on April 28, 2018.
Judith, ninety-seven, joined him hours later.
They had been married for seventy-two years.

Judith never forgot how lucky she was
to have survived the war.
She celebrated life
with parrots, pugs, and pixie dust,
in all their gleaming glory,
forever changing
the world of dressing up.
A world of magic in a handbag.

Author's Note

Judith Leiber liked to linger in the lobby of the Metropolitan Opera House and count how many patrons *weren't* carrying her handbags. It was a short list. Her bejeweled minaudières sparkled as brightly as diamonds—and cost nearly as much. But that didn't stop legions of women from buying them.

Famous divas everywhere clutched Leiber bags: Queen Elizabeth II, opera star Beverly Sills (who owned two hundred), actress Greta Garbo, singers Diana Ross, and Beyoncé, who toted a limited-edition Leiber bag (co-created with designer Alexander Wang) called "Show Me the Money" because it resembled a bankroll of cash!

So what if the bags could only hold, as Judith famously said, a credit card, a $100 bill, and a tube of lipstick!

Roominess wasn't the point. Judith's dazzling creations were all about showing off. Many are on display at the Smithsonian in Washington, DC, New York's Metropolitan Museum of Art, the Los Angeles County Museum of Art, and the Victoria and Albert Museum in London.

While Judith designed high-quality leather bags for day, as well as other accessories, her sparkly purses for night were the ones that made her famous, particularly a crystal-covered metal pouch made in 1967, which launched her fame.

Quality mattered to Judith, but so did sly humor. Why else make a purse that looks like a rattlesnake? Or an ice-cream sundae dripping with fudge? Or a bunch of asparagus?

Judith learned the business from the bottom up. She became the first female apprentice at Pessl, a prestigious handbag company in Budapest, where she rose to become a master craftsman. She went on to be the very first woman accepted into the craft guild in Budapest.

Perhaps most prestigious of all was her Lifetime Achievement Award given in 1993 by the Council of Fashion Designers of America, which celebrated her work throughout her long career.

Judith didn't *follow* fashion; she *made* it. But it didn't come easy. She worked long hours, chose not to have children, and devoted herself to what she loved to do best: create art. She was dubbed "the Fabergé of Handbags" because her jewel-like purses brought to mind the precious, gem-encrusted eggs made in Imperial Russia by the House of Fabergé.

Making objects of art was the focus of Judith's whole life. Even in her darkest moments, when she was a young girl held prisoner by the Nazis in Budapest, she could escape to a world in her head where beauty, joy, and creativity banished hate and oppression.

She never forgot how the power of imagination and the pursuit of dreams can carry one through adversity.

Bibliography

Nemy, Enid. *Judith Leiber: The Artful Handbag*. New York City: Harry N. Abrams, Inc., 1995.

Designer Judith Leiber Dies at 97
    wwd.com/accessories-news/handbags/designer-judith-leiber-dies-at-1202662640/

How Holocaust Survivor Judith Leiber Became a Handbag Legend
    townandcountrymag.com/style/g9267743/judith-leiber-handbags/

Judith Leiber Built Her Handbag Empire with Grit and Glitz
    1stdibs.com/introspective-magazine/judith-leiber/

Judith Leiber, 97, Dies; Turned Handbags Into Objets d'Art
    nytimes.com/2018/04/30/obituaries/judith-leiber-97-dies-turned-handbags-into-objets-dart.html

Judith Leiber, the Fabergé of Handbags, Has Died
    vogue.com/article/obituary-judith-leiber-handbag-designer

Judith Leiber: Fashion designer who escaped the Holocaust and went on to produce handbags for the stars
    independent.co.uk/news/obituaries/judith-leiber-dead-death-fashion-designer-handbags-holocaust-new-york-andy-warhol-a8382551.html

Leiber Collection
    leibermuseum.org

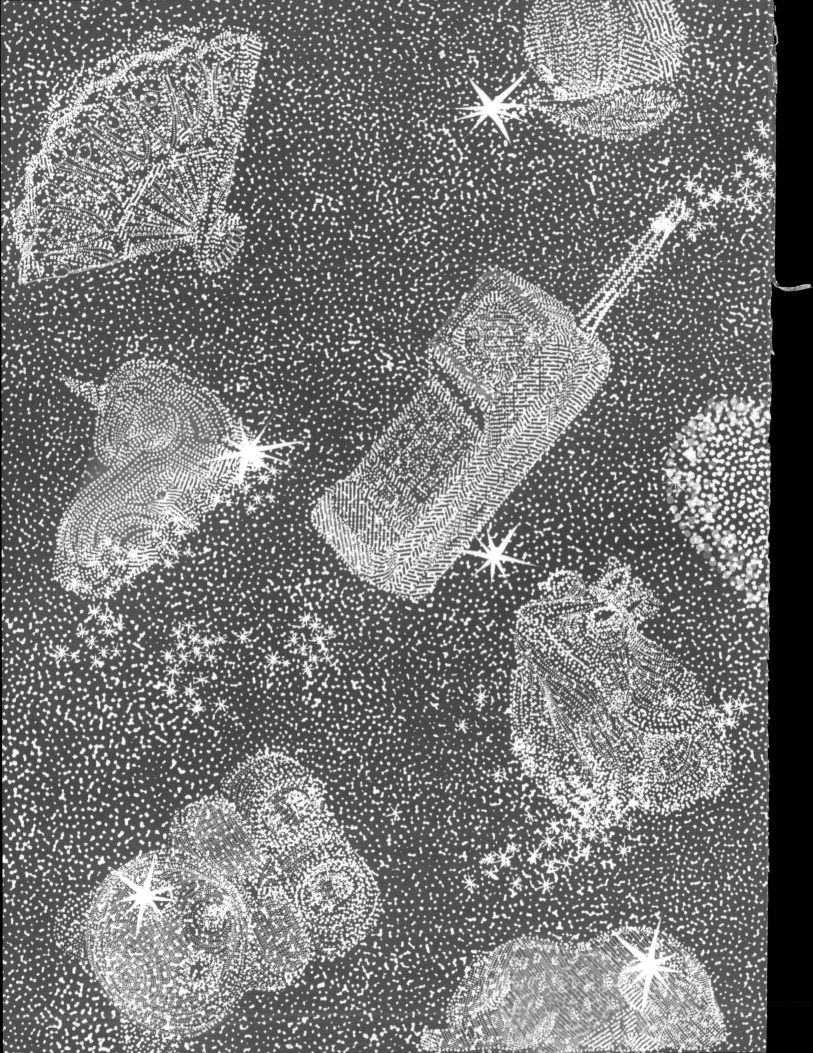